What More Could the Universe Want

Other works by Dennis Sampson

The Double Genesis

Forgiveness

Constant Longing

Needlegrass

For my Father Falling Asleep at Saint Mary's Hospital

Within the Shadow of a Man

The Lunatic in the Trees

Selected Poems

What More Could the Universe Want

poems

Dennis Sampson

Homestead Lighthouse Press
Grants Pass, Oregon

Copyright © Dennis Sampson, 2022. All rights reserved. No part of this book may be reproduced or transmitted in any form without the prior written permission of the publisher.

Library of Congress Cataloging-in-Publication Data
    Names: Sampson, Dennis, 1949-author.
    Title: *What More Could the Universe Want* / Dennis Sampson.
    Description: Homestead Lighthouse Press. Grants Pass, OR
    Homestead Lighthouse Press, 2019

ISBN 978-1-950475-30-8
Library of Congress Control Number: 2022948848

    Homestead Lighthouse Press
    1668 NE Foothill Boulevard
    Unit A
    Grants Pass, OR 97526
www.homesteadlighthousepress.com

Distributed by Homestead Lighthouse Press, Amazon.com, Barnes & Noble

Homestead Lighthouse Press gratefully acknowledges the generous support of its readers and patrons.

Book cover and interior design by Ray Rhamey, Ashland, OR

Contents

Stars over Shattalon Drive	1
The Monster That Ate Up Nothingness	3
Watching Fourth of July Fireworks from on Top of My House	4
Entering Eternity	6
Blake	7
Through the Hospital Corridor	10
Let Me Remember Instead	12
Summer Sequence	13
The Formalist	17
The Dance That Did Not Include Me	18
Evidence of Things Not Seen	19
Koi	20
On Being Put Up in the House of Phil Levine	22
Sunday at Saint Anne's Church with Dan	23
The Book of John	24
Song	25
Brittany	28
Speaking to the Recently Deceased	30
Making Love in Old Age Listening to Benny Goodman	36
Concluding with a Cliché	37
Spitting into the Mouth of Cassandra	39
The Russian	40
Those Beautiful People in the Room	42
The Rain	44
Rilke's Star	45
On This Planet Spun with Two Fingers	46
The Mole	48

Smoke	50
Brown Reeds, Woodpecker, Bull Frogs, Loon	52
Sources and Outcomes	54
Home	56
The Signature of Francisco Goya in the Corner of Saturn Eating His Son	57
Three Men in a Field	69
From Above	70
Homestead Lighthouse Press Interview with Dennis Sampson	72

for Nick, friend of many years

*Deep sky is, of all visual impressions,
the nearest akin to a feeling.*
          Coleridge, his notebooks

I have lost my way in the sky—-now, where?
          Osip Mandelstam

Stars over Shattalon Drive

Here for now, soon not to be here,
secret for now, not without purpose,
the stars over Shattalon Drive.
They changed when I wasn't aware
of their fervor,
though I kept my eyes open
at all times, their passion
for stillness a theorem to be studied.

There was this ungovernable
inward argument, as if my soul
were insomniac and kept tossing
about like a white miller in a mason
jar, caught drying between your thumb
and forefinger on the petal of
a jonquil, its guard down,
a restlessness that could not
be calmed so I could pay

close attention to its honesty. Those stars
allowed my eye to pass over,
like an insinuation of wind, insight
of a flashlight steered upward
by a daughter trying to find
a nightjar along a scrawl of water oaks,
the ardor of their longing impossible
to ignore. You are not a god

*even in your darker moments but you know
you know the difference
between here and there, there and elsewhere,
one far more frightening than the other,
just as it was for the Neanderthal
who looked up and grunted ontologically
at these same constellations
while urinating into a stream in Asia.*

The Monster That Ate Up Nothingness

Once upon a time there was a monster who liked to eat everything he saw. He was very hungry. So he ate the maple tree outside of town, the apple tree, and the oak. But that wasn't enough. So he stomped down to the pond and ate all the frogs, drank the water (scooping the fish into his mouth), and the rocks at the bottom of the pond. He rubbed his stomach, looked around at the world to see what else would please him—he saw clouds carried across the sky, reached up, grabbed them with his claw, GULP, they were gone. He ate all the rest of the trees in the forest and the flowers and the weeds. But he was still hungry. So he called the birds into his mouth, swallowed them, went into town and ate the houses—one right after the other. He ate the people too. But the monster was still famished even though he had eaten almost everything. His belly was as big as the world. "What else is there?" he wondered. He saw other monsters and he chased them down. Every last one of them. And he fornicated with every behemoth that he caught before he ate them up.

Then he started at one end of the world, worked his way to the other, gnashing till only he remained. He was still starved. So he ate one hand, then the other, then his whole hairy body. Nothing was left but the stars. These he ate too, although it took him awhile. The universe was darker and scarier than ever before. So he opened one more time like a hippopotamus yawning, put his mouth around NOTHINGNESS. His jaws flopped shut. That was that, although he was not happy. He wanted more, everything vanished except for what comes after NOTHINGNESS. And nobody can eat nothingness of course. But Oh there was something else. Hotter than fire. Crueler than truth. And that was his hunger. And his hunger ate up itself.

Watching Fourth of July Fireworks from on Top of My House

I'm a little frightened when there isn't any wind
on a night when fireworks over the Wart Hogs' baseball
stadium veer straight upward and pop like a paper bag
then drizzle down the sky,
sparks dwindling into the pastures north of High Point.

Frightened that I am not close to being a part of the revelry there,
the touched beer cups, the laughter, the bliss
at the end of the game seeing Roman Candles blossoming,
bottle rockets sizzling into center field
where the mascot slaps his baggy pants as if about to go up

in flames. I can clearly hear the husband dressed like Uncle Sam
ask where his wallet is before his wife points to her purse,
pulling it out to show him with a smile,
her auburn eyebrows lifted as if she knew full well who he is.
I hear the teenager with sparklers being chased with a scream

up the concrete aisle, crimson and yellow and orange
whacking against black sky, the awe
of everyone gazing up from the darkened left-field bleachers.
Little wind. An insinuating lift and shimmer, a little
persuasion of a summer breeze

threading the leaves. I am frightened, frightened.
Then this wave of anxiety
moving through me goes away like a stream.

It is only night. Not quite midnight.
Then the *weeeeeee* of another ascending parachute

lights the night sky. That pop again. Then a hush.
The wind is anticipating the right instant
to make itself experienced within those three tall hickories.
An intuition, a dread that lessens when I climb down

through the window and send myself off to sleep, dog fed,
dishes done, goulash in the refrigerator,
birds fed—all late coming to the feeder today for some reason—
letters stamped and laid on the table.
Afraid of something I can't put my finger on.

Entering Eternity

I am running as fast as I can
toward my final resting place, pushing everyone
else aside and even crawling over bodies
to get to the hole designated for me

where those who loved me are waiting, waiting,
checking their watches, fidgeting,
the smell of fresh dirt in their nostrils,
a sob here, a sob there, and all of them looking

over their shoulders at some point before the ceremony
for the corpse almost out of breath
to keep its appointment, saying "I'm sorry
I'm late" before hurtling
itself into the coffin,

going on about the traffic, the slick roads, blinding snow,
the accident that had cars backed up
for miles on the interstate. I am running,
to enter that eternity I've heard so much about.

Blake

His feet reek of vinegar
and he gawks with mouth open
when he sees something a little confusing
and turns his whole torso around.
I had a student who said to me
she was terrified of the elderly.
I told Rachel to get a job in a nursing home.
The young will never get old,
and the old will never be young again.
Eileen was gentle and fragile and aromatic
and after she put her coins
back into her purse she told the girl
behind the register she had a nice smile.
If you were a bastard all of your life
you'll be a bastard in old age.
The elderly do talk a lot about the weather.
And their purpose on earth no longer is
to make others have fun. Wisdom?
If they are wise they realize
the futility of offering any advice.
Their concept of money
after eighty years of pinching pennies
is way out of whack. My mother would
go to the grocery store and buy
two bananas and a pint of milk,
even though she had over a hundred
thousand dollars in her account.

Also, the elderly become invisible.
Nobody sees them anymore.
Or they look like cadavers wandering.
And the dread of death becomes curiosity
then something to look forward to.
Even Freud at eighty-one longed for non-being.
They wear tennis shoes. And Boston Red Sox
baseball caps that make them look dopier.
Opening a door for one
is miraculous. Helping them get groceries
they can't reach is too. They are gliding ghosts.
So much surviving
behind those surrendering eyes, heroic,
having lasted for so long
even though they now use portable toilets
and walk with agonizing slowness
so as not to trip and break a hipbone.
No insistence here, no motif, no theme.
Pressing my grandmother's Queen Anne's lace
to my nose and inhaling her death
set out so precisely on the antique table.
William Blake composing one last lyric
to his devoted wife on the day of his death.
My mother spent her final five years staring
through her wide window in assisted living
in her favorite blue chair in Minneapolis. "You just
have to get used to the fact, Linda," she said
to my sister, "I am going to die." Which she did
eight days after her stroke. I put my hand on her
forehead. She at ninety was no longer elderly.
I see these clueless Methusalahs with a cane.
I can tell from the worn handle

that cane has been their hand's companion for years.
They are not circumspect. They are forgetful.
I've seen them in hospital beds, on their backs, aghast,
rotten molars,
white hairs curling from nostrils and ears,
bed pans, IV's. Final simple statement:
my moral father saying to my moral mother
after some fifty years of marriage. "I have done
a lot of stupid things in my life, Lu,
but I have never been bad."

Through the Hospital Corridor

Bent over the resplendent old, doors left half open, name tags taped up saying Harriet and Edna and Archibald—orderlies in light blue smocks labor to console. There is only eternal daylight of fluorescent glow, so brilliant you could never hide from the illness constantly quarreling with the soul. Then that elderly voice, falsetto, that speaks with such precision of its dreadful plight—"help, help"—paired pleas repeated throughout the day, the night, as if to an intercessor nowhere to be found. The great grandmother raving on the phone deep in the interior stops talking. There is calm before the door swings inward showing the single bed, its railing turned down, with the yellow cotton blanket wrapped tightly, the single pillow, fluffed,

fresh linen for the patient soon to be admitted after being immobilized by a stroke potting geraniums with his daughter. And there are no days anymore for the octogenarian who loved to run her palm over the forehead of her dachshund that had leaped into her lap—only hours passed over by the rising, the setting sun—like a child lost in the dark—hours that don't belong to anyone. Then the pain breaks loose, and it races around like a mole sought by a Siamese cat in the garden after dark, diving headlong into its devious labyrinth. Hours become moments transformed into the long groan. It is timelessness now that turns the irrelevant hands of the Swiss watch first tried on in front of a mirror

in 1955, dangling from the bone of a wrist, timelessness stepping onto the ballroom floor in a floor-length gown, palm pressed firmly against the spine for the dip one has been waiting for, letting long blonde hair almost touch the linoleum, the slide and glide to Ellington's "Lotus Blossom." Solitary dancers stare into one another's eyes. Then the "help, help" again as though through a tunnel in the night, the lights of these monasteries turned off, turned down. "Help,

help"—the night nurse's laughter crescendos after the sneeze she has tried to stop. And the one who raved on the phone lies back staring up from on top of the covers, preparing for the argument of tomorrow falling toward the fact that is like no other.

Let Me Remember Instead

how still were the maples in the silence
of Wednesday night,
lamplight shining up into their long green gowns
from this window, how that star drew across the sky all other stars.

Justice is that tiniest roadside blossom closing up, and judgment
loves itself around the canister beneath the wind chime.

It comes
with the first hummingbird
in a rush. Has anyone ever atoned enough so we might fall

as effortlessly as a feather through what remains
rock hard? Mercy that brown moth widening paper-thin wings on
the wall

with oval spots, those four maples,
their stillness literally studied, rose geranium, ivy intertwined.

Summer Sequence

Hemlock father to the sea,
the sea in exodus, the sea blue-green,

green going dark brown now,
dark brown breathings cleared of leaves,

cooper hawk swooping
pursued by blackbirds from underneath,

the sun dreaming, not dreaming,
one cardinal, female,

staring directly up
at another, which looks down empathetically

*

no wind, a silence though
that listens, as it is listened to,

the sound of winter run-off
finding me in my sleep, scent

of honeysuckle in rain flying sideways,
sister to snow, brother to snow,

white fields of wheat,
the impossibility of speaking

and yet speaking easily, the freight train
working toward me on a bluff

overlooking the Missouri winding
away, the one thought that might

just be, what?—
seasons waited for, anticipated

*

then that slash of lightning
over Woonsocket, it is spring, spring,

scream of the blue jay, then sleep again,
what it means to do one perfect thing,

no one knows, as it has been
as it will be, the sun going down

methodically again, it is evening again,
earache, heartache, that ornate

bouquet this morning in the oncologist's
light blue mundane lobby, my memory of skating

gliding out into the outer reaches of the rink
at night at ten degrees,

scab on my knee, ringworm,
goldenrod, sawtooth sunflower, cicadas courting,

the baptistry on Sunday embraced
although strange, the washing

of brow and face and cheek, purification
of what is stained, original sin, God's grace

—then evening, not a single
chickadee in attendance in the hickory

*

the smell of earth on my dog's feet,
sawdust a good thing,

cherries, the seed spat into my hand,
grave after grave after grave

that is just witless,
anonymous, although named,

light at an angle, light everyplace,
relief (at not being), the enigma

the red fox might clarify,
bounding tomb to tomb today,

hard to explain—like my attraction
to rhubarb, snapped off, crunched

when I was perhaps thirteen,
eternity (everything okay), oblivion

constellations identified by my father
for me, for me, for me. I would like to go there

*

it is not to be, like Daphne's
changing into an unsuspecting laurel tree,

the return of love, love,
I tell myself this is mystery,

Zeus visiting Danae in her sleep,
as a golden shower in prison,

evening, it persists, it is released,
what I have to do tomorrow, MRI,

wisdom in the countenance of the linden
weighted down by today's late downpour,

linden that never goes anywhere,
stays where it is, thinking.

Humiliated, it will regain
great dignity. And be what it will be.

The Formalist

Almost everything he wrote
a pleasure to read, deftly executed,
always a little bit better
than expected. And he had the expertise

to reflect on what he witnessed
lackadaisically, his subjects simple—a sensible man
at ease in his blue love seat
with yellow legal pad, revising endlessly.

No visions. No metaphors. Few words
of wisdom, the image of an ancient
poplar releasing orange and yellow leaves
enough for him. Impeccable.

With an occasional scream. They said
he never got any better than his
first book, nor any worse. In the last
month of cancer, eschewing the prophetic

in favor of surrendering to the truth
of the bone scan, the hum of the ventilator,
he wished he could do it all again
with less pizzazz. Praise him.

The Dance That Did Not Include Me

Jane danced once and only once for me.
And what a dance it was, whirling around and around
her living room in a cotton dress and blouse to Beethoven's *Fidelio*,
uncoordinated, galloping up on the couch with her chin up
then in chaotic circles from the little white living room in Hills

to the kitchen and back to the living room again—delighted, delightful.
A mad ecstatic dance you could not practice unless by practice
you mean being bent over underneath the sink as a daughter
munching dog biscuits because a stepfather was blind drunk
and on the warpath—the whirling and swirling, and that wild smile

of someone kicking up her slippers this side of hell. I was in love. And I
was caught off guard by this dance that required no companion,
Beethoven in his shamelessness on the stereo, Jane's moving around
and through this slender delicate form that ricocheted
off the walls. For me, this was almost Eden.

Evidence of Things Not Seen

It's when I hear the Canadian geese I can't see
that a feeling of hope and good will
comes over me, that *ca-honk ca-honk ca-honk*
not so much the announcement of the end
or the beginning of a pilgrimage

but geese simply being who they are, geese,
that somehow aligned themselves in a V
with Caesar leading the way and were inclined
to pass right over me this evening. That ancient cry.
That cry of going forward

and of thanksgiving. So there they steer away
so I cannot see them, *ca-honk ca-honk*
on their way to Forsyth Cemetery. "I love geese" Ray Carver
mumbled at the party after his awful reading in Iowa City.

And I believed him. Beautiful their call
no matter what. Beautiful their being.

Koi

I see them
a trinity of independence
wavering
just under the surface,
one orange, the others what seem to be green,
long as a child's arm,
swaying so leisurely they might be somnambulists
or they themselves the dream
of being well beyond words that would explain
that interim between life
and what we have no capacity to understand.
And I wonder what these three must
be thinking along the bottom of the pond
in midwinter when the geese have
long been gone, a film of ice
pocked by rocks thrown out,
that spreads outward along the shoreline.
Wonder if their communicating in a way
unavailable to us is realistic,
never very far apart,
Camus, Sartre, Simone de Beauvoir.
I notice them walking by my lonesome self
Sunday mornings
and think about their couldn't-care-less
camaraderie—this lazy trinity.
Without the slightest inclination
to get away. Or to even quiver a little

when like a kid I flip a twig
between
those slow monotonous poltergeists
expecting nothing
of anyone except their desire to be together.

On Being Put Up in the House of Phil Levine

"Fucking goddamn heart" I heard that irascible man say
after he got up from his nap, and I ran over
and over in my mind throughout that afternoon
the syntax of that sentence and how it seemed to exemplify
his life. Golden the fallen oranges on the lawn,
the garden in disarray and his wife's determination
to dig and uproot—golden the light around her modest paintings
in the small garage. I was looking for a job
and found in the late hours at a faculty party
I was out of the running, so turned my thoughts
to those couplets by Jarrell called "The House in the Wood"
that I asked that truth teller to search his bookcase for
for its "We are far under the surface of the night."
Of all the things I saw in Fresno I remember best
mountains that insisted on being pointed out,
their summits covered in new snow,
and the poet's getting up that afternoon dressed
in his old blue Nikes saying "Fucking goddamn heart."

Sunday at Saint Anne's Church with Dan

What a day. Someone poked
my arthritic elbow at the supermarket this afternoon
to remind me to take my Visa credit card
I had forgotten on the counter.
And this morning at Saint Anne's I turned begrudgingly

when everyone was asked by Father Fallin to say something welcoming
to those in front and behind of and beside them. And getting up
behind me one old so-thin widow
dangled out her blue-veined hand. Her eyes the deepest green.
I pressed her frosted palm I will never press again.

Dan, who had not had a drink in decades and who always
turned up the volume in his Cadillac Seville's car radio
when I hummed, and talked with his hand cupped
surreptitiously over his cell phone
looked up almost moronically as if he had been through this

a zillion times. I've come a long way—that fragrance
of ancient perfume on my hesitating hand.

The Book of John

It took a lifetime for him to simply say "I quit."
Then an idea came to him like a daughter that had asked

her father to dance, and that father stepped out shyly
onto the ballroom floor because why in the world

would you ever want to say no to someone as happy as that?
That idea offered the possibility of metaphor,

his scribbling in the dirt just as Christ
did while being besieged by insidious little questioners

the morning Linda Kaulda from across Riverview Avenue
was embraced by flames running and crackling up along her night-
gown

after playing with matches on the stairs,
her shrieks he had not thought to imagine at the time

rattling the china in the cabinet. So he took
out his pen and wrote with the commitment

of a boy assembling the mechanism of a wristwatch.
And the word *angel* came to him, the word *flame*, the word *risen*.

Song

1.

To see someone you love lifted from the swung doors of
an ambulance then rushed through gradually parting glass doors

of a hospital in Birmingham isn't the end of getting up to turn
on the lights around the front window in late December, those blue

and crimson and white lights that celebrate the birth of a mastermind
so far advanced he could recite the alphabet in every dialect ad infinitum.

2.

Death throws back its black flashing hair
and positions its palm up under the neck, gently,

as if cradling a baby, rubbing with its finger the lips
with analgesic and examining those round auburn eyes

like the eyes of someone under the influence of mescaline.
The oncologist, distant, inquisitive, flicks dandruff

from the shoulder of his lab coat before turning his slender
back to walk the hospital lobby with his computer open. Death

answers to everything. That stench, translucent as a glimmer
of rain hesitating at the tip of a magnolia leaf, belligerent,

sometimes even sweet, whispering into one's tilted ear,
death the smell of shit in the gymnasium restroom

and the twang of a tire iron hitting concrete,
those trembling fingers of the elderly electrician

who can't get his key to fit, death the intruder
steering the beam of his flashlight through a window

sliding across the statue of St. Francis holding close a lamb
on the mantle above the fireplace,

that too-human song of the castrati and the afterbirth
of an unwed secretary on her back in an elevator in Queens,

her clenched face held up by a stranger stroking her
cheek telling her everything will be okay—hang in there.

3.

I was alone. I had seen death crouching,
seen the muscles flex and listened to death's breath

like that of one who has just stopped running,
panting with its hands on its knees while others

screamed to others to go in another direction. I have to say
the loveliness of that woman lifted in the last

stage of breast cancer was something I was not
remotely prepared for. Ghost, monster, courtesan,

wind flipping over a brown hickory leaf then flipping it
back again, minister, the pungent odor of urine

hissing into a fire at night and the emergence
of a deity from between sprawled white thighs,

what in truth you are, and why,
wintering out your solitude in silence

and holding your glass up for a toast
at a cocktail party given in honor of that other birth,

in Birmingham, Kurdistan, in Guatemala,
deity to those coming in, to those going out.

Brittany

You were wonderful and lit up
in the white dress you lifted a little
so as not to trip. Your cheeks blushed,
almost too beautiful to see

when you at last clambered down, without touching
the railing, awkwardly the staircase
that evening in May,
a little too much Chanel #5 perhaps

but that was okay. And there
would be years to come before
your stillborn child, your horrible divorce,
ovarian cancer with chemotherapy

and radiation that turned you bald and,
strangely, more beautiful to me
than I remember
when you stepped down to me that evening in '68.

Sleep
with the same man for nearly twenty-three years,
a Kenmore salesman who snored and bantered in Spanish
when he dreamed—three kids. You called them near

your deathbed at Druid City Hospital to say
you loved them all
with nowhere to go for once
in this gullible world. Here's to you who referred

to what you were going through as "Mommy's cancer,"
your moans suppressed so as not to scare your kids.
Your daughter Molly left purple lipstick on your anemic cheek
to take with you into the life after this.

Speaking to the Recently Deceased

It doesn't mean they are listening.

*

Close your eyes
on a Friday night after you've seen a sickle moon
you appreciated,
as if the two of you were dreaming,
and speak
self-consciously to the wife whose leukemia
emptied her completely in three days.

*

I was too anesthetized to scream.

*

The way introspective Stephanie fiddled with her bangs
when she was thinking.

*

You can go on talking if you want
as if
she lay there beside you in the night

after a day when you had a confrontation
with a colleague that still bothers you.

*

Don't ask for advice. That's
where the dead draw the line,
their silence as refined
as any god who taught them this poker face
when someone is being tortured
or falling out of the sky.

*

Talking to the dead is done all the time,
often without moving the lips,

like a thought passed on like warm bread
at a table set for a dozen.

*

How you decided
to give up on the flower garden that won't respond
to anyone else's touch.

*

Poetry no longer a form of prayer.

All deities dead.

Greater men than I have asserted such.
But aren't the dead talking?

*

When words come flying out I rush to scribble them
down, like the student who writes
frantically when I lecture on what I'm guessing
about what Emily Dickinson means seeing a serpent in the grass.

Obsession with the afterlife. That non-thing.
Or are you actually
praying distractedly for those who have no voice now,
Dickinson among them?

*

Who was it said the only two topics
for the poet are eroticism and death?
Yeats, if I remember correctly:

subjects connected like coupling water moccasins
I haven't the heart to discuss

only to say

the erotica of the flesh
is never more evident than in the elderly

being bathed—their heads bowed—
with soft yellow sponges and warm wet washcloths

because they can't
get out of bed.

*

In good time
I too will be talked to as though my face
were turned away

and either hear the solemn conversation
of one who wants me

to be deaf to the words that are said
in the night, or not, light off, an act of faith

so powerful I too almost open
my mouth, then want no part of this.

That is if I have a face

which I doubt

mine

gone to dust
along with everything else in a coffin

that gets up every morning exactly at sunrise
and totters around awkwardly as if

all things were possible—
as long as mystery and longing are coterminous

*

the British Shorthair stuffed with cotton and left advancing
on the mantel,
the stance of mumbling mourners, heads bowed,

hands linked, eyes shut,

waiting for word from the other
they hope doesn't hold a grudge
exorcisms, summonings

*

God may be passe
but that doesn't mean He hasn't
a trick or two or three up His sleeve,

gun in hand, so to speak.
From the beginning of time He has been waiting
to squeeze the trigger,

such restraint, such patience we have never seen,
the barrel after eons and eons
lifted until it is pressed meaningfully
against the temple

and the dead
who don't listen, or listen disinterestedly, at best,
to petitions made on the knees,

go on speaking
to he who weeps, he who continues to need.

Making Love in Old Age Listening to Benny Goodman

I wish I could find just one good love poem
of someone in his eighties,
one that addresses uninhibited cravings, foreplay for sure,
one that perhaps is written
as if the loved one were miles away at sea.

Urgency is what I would look for,
as it was for Andrew Marvell in his persuasive
solicitation that threatens his lover with decrepitude
if she should deny his devilish
eloquent request to ravish her from bottom to top.

Old flesh, tender bones, liver spots, stale breath,
teeth that have turned yellow and quirks
that make it challenging, to say the least
for such an encomium to be composed
by those who know nothing about sleeping

next to one another for nearly half a century.
Close your eyes and see them tentatively caress,
call out one another's first name softly
in a room illuminated by sandalwood candles,
Benny Goodman letting it rip on the stereo, his alto

clarinet lifted high. Simultaneous orgasms. Then
the lying there one on top of the other, out of breath,
pallid bodies in the dim boudoir, euphoria subsiding
over the course of what seems like a millennium.

Concluding with a Cliché

So much of what I wanted no longer
possible anymore. Or wanted anymore. A
night and a day with Jane, a strong fire snapping
its whips in the dark while we sat on her sofa
and simply stared—that would still be good—
talking in low tones so as not to disturb
the ghosts we were in the process
of becoming while the years flowed
over and through the holiness
of hearing my name called out from another
part of the house. It always bothered me
when Jane spoke with her back turned and she
didn't like that I often had to ask twice
because she mumbled. Still, a day
and a night, nothing more than that, and maybe
that moon at twilight again over the Missouri
drinking cheap Merlot from the bottle
after ringing the bell of an abandoned church
we'd broken into on the plains, and cattle close
to the fence, drooling but far from stupid, extending
their tremendous heads through barbed wire
to get the greenest grass—and that
night in New York City too reading Dante
at the Cathedral of Saint John the Divine
from the lectern, with Jane and Louie, and the laughter
after smoking pot in the seminary gardens
before the Easter service. What does

not seem too much to ask is still asked for,
this time only once, the response
forthcoming as if it were listened to from across
a river at night, complete with the full moon,
as clear as any bell I have ever heard.

Spitting into the Mouth of Cassandra

That most modest of songs, Eberhart,
in no more than two deftly executed stanzas
showcasing the image of a lamb
in my first literature class

putrifying on a green hillside. I remember that poem so well.
My own little mythological wanderings. Oh well.
Cassandra
savoring the taste of god's saliva
spat into her wide open mouth.

Richard Eberhart, "For A Lamb"

The Russian

Thinking back, this midsummer evening,
Vodka and tonic in hand, of what happened at the reception

after the reading when the music was cranked up and all
those MFA students began to swirl and jerk

around Brodsky while he sat hunched over
on the couch, flailing their arms. I don't remember

much of Brodsky's reading, although
I know he didn't read his poems in Russian

and that he was extremely serious, even solemn,
as if he were considering whether to throw himself

from a bridge over the Volga or go on living.
He had been through something similar

to Mandelstam and his early
lyrics were recognized for their searing

eloquence by Ahkmathova
who had her own idea of what it means

to be hunted down. Then banishment. Then the
frivolity of America and all that attention. I stood

right behind Brodsky and looked at his pale bald head
when cautious Dara asked if he would like

to dance, extending her slender feminine arm, and I
waited for his reaction, imagined him doing the frug

after all he had been through, to which Brodsky,
as profoundly as an old toad tired of being nudged

with a thumb, hunched over, sullenly said "No, I don't do
dance," then sat there suffering in his pea-green suit

over what had come to pass for him at the University of Alabama
after agreeing to read of his being in exile from us all.

Those Beautiful People in the Room

I haven't written anything since February
I tell the last class of the month, *but that's no reason
to panic*—then give the lecture on patience,
preparations for the miraculous words that descend.

*Keep a notebook handy. You could be
washing dishes or just lying awake in bed
when Wham you're writing down everything.*
The question for the day pertains

to their most vivid image of the natural world,
and Nicky says "poppies out of nowhere"
and Ashley says "monarch butterflies
blown off course I found near the shore,"

Keeko, chattering too fast about hallucinating
on mushrooms, on his back on a football field in Houston.
Elena: "There's this Georgiana
Holly outside my window all dressed up

with spider webs," and Tricia, "waiting
for the horses to come in when I was a kid
at sunset turning all golden,"
and Katherine "summer thunder from a solitary cloud."

Diane: "Looking down off the coast near Santa Cruz."
"There's this pasture I used to pass" says Vanessa
that had one cow in the corner,"
then talks of coming upon the farmhouse of a friend

surrounded by dozens of them,
and I tell her write "How I Am Going To Get The Cows
Back Into The Pasture," which makes her happy
and she begins writing madly. Late summer. 1976.

Dusk. I'm in the stands
while my ex-wife takes the field
for the Luckey Bluebirds,
heartbreaking in her awkward jog across the infield,
the first time I'd seen her run like that.

when Robyn softly responds
"I woke my sister up that night I saw so many
stars from the backyard." But I'm remembering Margaret
chasing the fly ball sailing to left
and wondering *Where should I begin?*

"The black dirt of Minneapolis" Amy chimes in
as if with a koan, and I'd give anything
to have that moment back
listening to the crack of the bat and the cry
of the rising crowd. I'd give anything to have that back.

The Rain

What of the long cold nights of stars over the prairie,
of the mornings drifting with mist.
What of the sun over the farmhouses and towns and fields,
of that light changing in the leaves of the sole tree,
of what runs like wind through the water meadow,
of what rages, then forgets its rage.
What of that big book open to Ezra's death mask in Venice,
of that book open to Ezra's death.
What of the book closed. Of the book left out overnight
in the pouring rain, the pages soaked.
What of the days, months, seasons. Sweet Jesus.

Rilke's Star

That one star stationed way out there?
It's one Rilke looked up to after acknowledging
the treacherous passage
of time and how we often treat one another so badly,

mysterious inhabitant

of the cosmos Galileo
excitedly identified and that ruffled all of the feathers of
the Holy Office. So clear. Uncorrupted. Offering itself
to be thought about, tilting vertiginously eastward

along with

those dimming dead others. If you can't appreciate the pressure
Rilke puts on that star
to stand for something to believe in
I don't know what to tell you.
It requires courage. It requires more than anything else

an open heart.

On This Planet Spun with Two Fingers

How little I knew then, how heartbreakingly naïve
to include a blood-red tulip in the new snow
right after I got home and that
I'd seen in very early April at Stephanie's,

all those disclosures of a life yet to be lived
except for the childhood along a slow brown river.
Such innocence. And yet I'd be a fool to turn my back
on those secrets that told me who I was, would be,

even if I was unaware of all this in my naivety–
innate sorrow and the subject of the brevity
of this life underscored by the love I felt seeing a barefooted
little girl in a white dress one summer running toward

her mom twisting her hands around in a dishrag,
shouting for Elizabeth to come in from the swing set
for her favorite meal of mashed potatoes. I loved. But I also knew
the cards were stacked against us on this planet spun

by two fingers in elementary school one nostalgic afternoon,
bringing that smooth globe to a halt
with one touch, and discovering where
I lived in the universe until Mrs. Freiburg told me to go

to my desk in the back of the class that had so many
names carved into it. My hands were folded. I waited for the directive
to go to the blackboard that went wall to wall and write
one hundred times *I will not get out of my seat without permission.*

The Mole

I know what you're thinking. That this is just
a journey through the dark
leading to knowledge only a mole
would know what to do with. When it is day

for you it is night, striving beneath
the cocktail party on the patio pushing up mounds.
Everyone there wonders what to do with you
and your wife. You do have a wife,

don't you? Does she not often find you
snoring in your sleep in one of the innermost
tunnels, curled up, tufts of dust
blossoming upward with each diminutive puff?

Does she not let you rest? How hard
being the architect
of labyrinths you yourself often get lost in
now and then, squinting, an aficionado of grit

bumping up against roots, fence posts,
coffins. Blind burrower,
nemesis of the grub, star-nosed groper
hurrying to and fro, you are the great seeker,

self-absorbed, until thunder shakes the foundations
of your world and your question "Who is there?"
becomes the requisite response
of others doomed to dig beneath the earth.

Smoke

I caught a whiff of cigarette smoke
from across Echo Lake—an old
Afro-American woman in pink leotards fishing
with two fiberglass poles from her lawn chair,
the handle of one of them thrust
into the earth, one gripped by her casual hand.
And don't you know suddenly it was fifty years ago
and Jimmy Osberg who had filched Marlboros
from Rexal's drugstore, eyes flashing left,
eyes looking right, was puffing away in summer
with me on the summer lawn
beside Rigg's high school. Jim's dead now,
of emphysema, and keeps popping up
in my dreams. I tried to call him
before he died. No answer. No answering machine.
But it is a beautiful day today in the dead center
of March and my dog for once doesn't yank
on his leash, why I don't know, even seems
to investigate the wet rocks and fallen branches
reflectively, wisteria so yellow, particularly against
the background of gray winter maples.
I'm not going to lie to you. This saddens me.
If time is not the ultimate mind fuck
then I don't know . . . Jimmy, you are more
than welcome to inhabit my dreams
but if given the opportunity would you please
find it within yourself to chase my

my last wife away with a flaming broom?" The day lilies—
they burst assertively into orange in the front
of my cottage. I should take myself out
there and look at those familial beauties.
Then there is that identifiable scent
sailing across the lake this afternoon.
Who is to say my life was meaningless?

Brown Reeds, Woodpecker, Bull Frogs, Loon

He saw them in the third month of the year,
all in one day, although the frogs were merely a gulp

as they withdrew to avoid the very eye that had brought
him to this point. The woodpecker shot straight up,

braced itself on the maple, flashing that patch of blood,
its posture perfect while it pounded away. The reeds

shuddered in the breeze. Then he heard the loon,
that hysterical and lonely laughter, and saw its silhouette,

too small to be a goose, too big to be a duck,
far out on the wrinkled surface of the pond. NO

TRESPASSING was something none of them
had to attend to, that wooden sign driven deep

in sludge years ago by someone accustomed to
the pleasures of the negative. Later he carried them

all inside his head, ate and slept with them,
watched them when he closed his eyelids,

introducing a little sunlight after awhile
that showed where the pond was shallow,

giving greater definition to the shoreline,
and later a moon that seemed to heighten

the hilarity of the loon, the solemnity of the frogs.
No boats. Not a single canoe. Innumerable flakes

of gold though, and a single light from a window
in a house painted blue. The woodpecker

flicked its blood up into the trees repeatedly
and the reeds took on a hint of green. This

was good. This is what he wanted. The mind has
an eye just like that which watches winter turn

to spring and the bullfrogs wince underwater.
The mind has an eye. And so does the soul.

Sources and Outcomes

Too many moons crossing in solitude
the landscape of the heart,
too many crooked strokes of lightning
giving the cottonwoods their singularity again
and the wind preceding the thunderstorms,
your terrified brow beaten dog seeking sanctuary
under the bed you both have
slept in for years. Now the mother I knew

is scarcely known in memory anymore,
her slippers paired perfectly on her side
of the double bed under which our Spaniel quivers,
my father with his wife's tacit consent lingering
now and then over an unrealistic female in
Playboy, flipping the pages
after pausing on his back first here, then there,
too many memories of the living
that seemed as if they all were so many eulogies,

Uncle Harlan's death for example
that I dramatized in a handwritten letter
to Larry and that was preparation for one's
own distant death—what frightens us
as prolonged thunder does the
Spaniel whose shoulders shudder under the bed.
Valhalla. Uncle's massive heart attack.
Our world's wars.

      And for me
the three quarters moon over the cool cool prairie
and fragrance of sage on the hillside
above a river shimmering like broken glass
that flows through the heart that knows,
that can't articulate its secret no matter how
many times it finds its way into words,

the feeling of the slick wind above the river in Chamberlain
swaying a long row of silver birches
while it pursues a piece of reckless cellophane
up against a barbed wire fence. Beginning
and end. Sources and outcomes.
Impossible to tell apart.
The intuition and the labor that led you
here to a solitary house here in mid-winter.

Home

I had given it one hundred and ten percent. The early bird
caught the worm. And the fact of the matter was
I even put my nose to the grindstone once
or twice. Adiós. So long. Goodbye. Muchas gracias.

I was primed to push the envelope, make my case,
cut to the chase, lay everything on the table.
So I pressed the pedal to the metal. I was off.
A bat out of hell. No turning back. I was history. Not

a single stone left unturned. Every nook
and cranny. I'd made my peace with the Lord
and had let bygones be bygones. I was dead
as a hammer. I was pushing up daisies, kaput,

had bought the farm, kicked the bucket, was buried
with my boots on, definitely six feet under. And then
I heard your voice, melodious, as clear as clear
can be, so beautiful and true, calling me back home.

The Signature of Francisco Goya in the Corner of Saturn Eating His Son

And I know it is easier to forgive the cruelty
of a stupid man than a man who knows exactly

what he is doing. I know the most
devout follower does not know God as He really is

anymore than the astronomer knows the cosmos,
that looked at long enough, the human eye

offers the kind of contentment that otherwise
comes only from prayer, that Diogenes

was reincarnated as a mockingbird
and the eyes of the cat do not belong to the cat.

I know the spider that has spun a web
under the sink has found its way up into the kitchen

by slow degrees and that man moves in a dream
from which he wakes intermittently, that love

and lust struggle to discover a country
in which they can both live peacefully. And I know

when the last living thing is gone from the cosmos
death will feast off its memories.

    . . . . .

I know too that the wisest man feels inferior to those he sees
through the eyes of their creator. And that it is hard
to be human, that one is at the mercy of one's appetites

and a child hugging another child when they think
nobody is looking is love that should leave
the deepest skeptic breathless. And that it is disquieting

to go for my morning walk knowing the blue heron
along the pond is watching and that the turtle sunning on the log
sees me coming too close in and drops out of sight just when I

look up, that there is nothing more pitiful
than a mother who defers to the authority of her child
and the elephant has a rump only another elephant could love.

    . . . . .

I know that mankind should exchange places
with the animals at the zoo and the monkeys

should look at us, that ultimately
the only thing that matters is the red abandoned barn of my childhood,

that even the smell of shit would become acceptable
if we associated it with someone we love, that the murderer

and the mystic are one and that a good man can easily be ground
down by fear to an eerie snitch. I know that the dullard is a dead executive

with bad breath who keeps climbing out of his grave to lecture us
on heaven, and that all over America right now

office workers are daydreaming wildly at their desks.

. . . . .

I know the desire to know has its price,
that the beetle has only its stink to keep people away

and that one shouldn't go into the forest unless one knows
one way or the other if the witch is there,

that when God screamed the dead shut up,
and the doorway to paradise is always through the human heart,

that a dog knows that its bite hurts
and the difference between someone who says Father

and someone who says God is immense,
that men who can't swim catch big fish

and that if we get far enough into the abyss
we will run into Rilke.

. . . . .

I know a soul in hell is tormented with the worst
possible thoughts without actually going mad, that even

the Buddha winces with an abscessed tooth, and that hate
faces away from the gates of Elysium. I know as well the alphabet

concludes with a deep sleep and that if one broods over the world
the sun still comes up and clouds fly overhead without giving

thought to this, that the solitary maple tree in late autumn
seems so beautiful at night when the light from the street lamp shines

on its leaves, and that when the tiniest bird sings sweetly
in the evening, who is to say it isn't really screaming?

And that it is hard to reconcile oneself to the fact
someone you once loved knows the meaning of everything

in death, that looking at the horror and having the horror
look at you are significantly different experiences,

that my eyes staring at my eyes in the mirror is frightening
and although you wouldn't think unrequited love

would make a difference in a universe as big as this
it does. I know that we see just how small the human being is

at noon with the sea behind him. And I love to listen to people
when they whistle because it is like suddenly hearing the Dalai Lama

in the midst of chatter and sounds so much like the truth.

. . . . .

I know the best definition of the afterlife
is the sense of someone waiting for you in an adjoining room,
that the dead look at the dead and accept them

with such sympathy, that although the
solo of the cricket
is exquisite, the trees still thrash and yearn.
And that anyone who buries his nose in a rose is an angel.

The chickadees in the hickory, the mysteries in the mystery,
the mystery rooted in the mystery spinning
through the mystery of space.

Do you seek the truth? Get directions to the
butcher's house.
He knows it like the back of his hand.

  . . . . .

And I know that when the sun goes down the sun
is already beginning to push up on the horizon,

that the brown orb weaver at the exact
center of its web is an illustration of good and evil

united in one unknowable mind and that fear is flipping through
the pages of the Psalms even as I speak, that happiness hears

what it wants to hear, my eyes flutter when I am lying,
and the only thing Christ couldn't do on the Cross

was look behind. I know the grave is moving at great speed
while we wait in line for the usher to take our ticket

and that what goes slowly goes its own way
while what quickens requires slick, invisible destinies,

that everyone who has ever spoken to the dying in soft tones
remembers to check the stove before they leave for the evening. And that God

is a long watch over a blue and wandering wind, and everyone thinks
of redoing the dishes when they are feeling guilty. I know

eating alone is nothing more than the need to turn and ask
Judas Iscariot what he really thinks and that Saint Augustine

must have really hated his mother Monica,
that Blaise Pascal had a first name equal to this evening.

    . . . . .

Give me that swatch of moonlight in the unmoving spruce.
Give me the nude moon, the naked breeze.
The signature of Francisco Goya in the corner of *Saturn Eating His Son*,
the cricket indifferent to me.

Give me the single bark of a solitary collie after dark
while I sip my dry martini and think.

    . . . . .

And I know the quarreling of two crows over the corpse
of an opossum will conclude as it began and that the old shoe

riding a piece of driftwood is searching for Ithaca, that evening
has its own song just as dawn has its own minuet and afternoon

its ruses, that abstinence seeks the same information as gluttony
and the politician who closes his eyes when he is praying

is playing a little game—that between getting up and lying down
a journey has occurred that will be remembered only

for its bluebirds and the woman who flipped back her black hair
at the supermarket. And I think Christmas Eve and Halloween

are the only holidays on speaking terms, that the ducks
on the pond are mocking the master of ceremonies at a convention

for the elimination of pencils and paper clips and the caterpillar
crossing the highway by the lake has no idea, that no bone

has ever fallen out of any sky, and that my father
in death couldn't possibly be so reticent.

    . . . . .

And I wonder if God hides in the wine the way a child
pulls the covers up over her face, and in the bread with the secret

syllable that must be spoken only in complete silence,
and if the ghost in the machine is fazed at all when a cluster bomb takes out

a semicircle of school children and a Pakistani woman slits
her throat. I wonder too if when it is night

the full moon over Jerusalem is the same moon
that glimmered on the crematory roofs at Bergen-Belsen and how many times

the hummingbird at my feeder realized it is an analogy for the finger
that dared to caress the long jagged scar of the mastectomy

performed three weeks after a good laugh over eggs and bacon.
I wonder when the world closes in if what doesn't exist for us

opens out and shouts loudly in a language soon to be learned
for its disappearing verbs and fugitive nouns on their knees singing.

Father to sorrow, father of grief,
fellowship of wren and cardinal and chickadee,

I have eaten the good meat
and fallen asleep on the patio with my feet up again.

. . . . .

And I know, in addition, that it is difficult to enjoy your veal
under a disciple's increasingly judgmental stare from across the table

and that the blast furnaces of Hell serve no other purpose
than to satisfy the imagination of the famished fundamentalist

munching his way page by page through Revelation,
that the unattainable follows us around like the shadow we cast

when we are trying to catch the cat. I know the face
of the forensic psychiatrist has assimilated each and every devious

lifting of the eyebrows and comes away from the gyrations
of the lie with the countenance of an archangel

who doesn't take any shit, that you too
must have amorous daydreams threading the needle

that will sew the yellow coral button back on the coat
passed onto you from your father. I know reading Emily Dickinson

is like having a concubine scratch your back while at the same time
undergoing a Chinese torture test, that the wish to be invisible as a kid

is fulfilled in late middle-age for the husband in tight trunks with an erection
in the public swimming pool telling everyone to come on in, that the wren

that can't find its way out of the house is Thomas Stearns Eliot
told he got it wrong from start to finish.

And I love the appearance of impropriety on the staid scholar's face
when he is dragged out of the nineteenth century and is asked to sit down

at the dinner table where not a single drop of claret is served,
love the dungeon you catch glimpses of when the emperor at eighty

opens his rotten mouth, love the use of nocturnal to describe
a bird and the reverie of three aspens in sunlight above the bridge.

I love the holiness of stones seen under the surface of a stream
that carries a leaf along as if it were the history of what those stones

were thinking and that the agony of an old birch humiliated by the evangelist
of the wind during a Sunday thunderstorm that blackens the nave

leaves the parishioners muttering uneasily. I love, too,
the hands that separate when a light pole comes between them

then find their way back to whisper what they went through in the interim
and I can't think of anything more revealing than two skeletons

conversing on a stone bench outside that house on Windsor Avenue
and the shuddering ghosts that haunt the evergreens on Halloween.

. . . . .

And I am troubled by the heretic hunting the mouse
with the determination of a woman scouring the pockets

of her spouse when he leaves to pick up their new TV at Walmart,
troubled by what it was that made Isaac Newton take a look up

at the moon right after that apple had fallen,
by the child that glances sideways instead of turning her head,

the blueish alstroemeria blossoms enamored of late light
and the ant that carries a crumb across my counter like a trophy.

I am troubled by what the swallows at twilight
are elegantly designing while they stitch and steer through the sky,

by the universal praise of the female cardinal always protesting
the nihilist's caw, the cynic's black arched eyebrow,

and I must know the answer right now to the question Gerard Manley Hopkins
asks in his fourteener "Pied Beauty" about everything that is freckled,

must know how something comes of nothing and what
accounts for the wisdom of the mud turtle at the bottom

of the pond, and why the root of the live oak displays
such extraordinary patience wrapping its roots around the coffin

of a father remembered for his love of all the larks in his garden.

. . . . .

And when it is night the expanding universe leans down
like a lumberjack trying to tie his boot and sunrise never tires

of itself and the Siamese cat licking the underside of its thigh
doesn't care one way or the other if we have an opinion, and evil

argues only insofar as it knows that its rhetoric will be wasted on
the bachelor that mows around the wildflowers in his yard

and mercy never measures the distance
and compassion has the right to put its foot down in the darkness

just as decisively as a solid block of granite
commands the religious fanatic to answer the question.

. . . . .

Something momentous, something tiny,
a rip along the hemline of a cotton dress,

the scream, someone beginning to run,
the pause between universe beginning,

universe finished, and what happens after that,
motive and act, cause and effect,

everything it seems a means to an end,
God the Father, God the crab

vanishing immediately backward into the sand,
the spear hurled sideways across black sky

on a night when you scribble without whiskey
bent over like an embryo at your desk.

Three Men in a Field

One looks one way, the other another.
One faces the setting sun
above a scarlet cloud above a mountain,
the others what light does
on grass cropped by black and white cattle,
of the same mind—one and the same.
They are three grateful daylilies,
wet with dew.
They are shadows
of a cross, and where their darknesses unites
a fragment of light
shines for a while in thought.

Give them everything they want
in the time that survives,
divine and otherwise.
Not only must the prospect of another dawn
forgive their always being lost
but instruct them
on what comes carefully again,
first crimson, then golden to the eye.
And if these three remain
as they are, what will become of
a life lived out in silence
with all the constellations, one looking up,
one down, one all around?
What more could the universe want?
Three men in a field is enough.

From Above

Rained last night. Now a couple of ducks paddle
in still shallows. The current is swift and pours
smoothness over the boulders and swirls
along the shoreline as if it were uncertain
as to where it were going. The male knows
someone's up here, so does the following female,
both holding their place, though, before
allowing the force of water to sweep them out
assertively sideways, like someone struggling
to walk straight in a stiff wind, up onto a tangle
of leaves and branches. Their snow-white tails flicker
and the speculum on each of their wings glints in the sun's light.
I'm sorry. They love each other. It's so obvious.
It is like watching William and Dorothy Wordsworth
on one of their walks while they wait for Coleridge
to stop talking, which he does, directly, leaving
them to speak privately of Coleridge's weirdness after
he has turned back. Could be these two mallard ducks
are still courting. Could be they have already expressed
their vows. Either way their camaraderie is very deep.
Then the mottled female flashes under the little bridge
and glances up while that luminescent green male stays
right where he is. Clearly they have an understanding
concerning what to do whenever humans intervene.
"Quack-quack" says William. "Rhab-rhab" Dorothy
answers back. "Quack-quack" "rhab-rhab" "quack-quack."

Interview

Conducted by Homestead Lighthouse Press
11/27/2022

Who or what inspired you to become a poet?

My mother was a voracious reader of decent literature--no romance novels and the like--and would sit in her recliner by the living room window with Hemingway's A FAREWELL TO ARMS or Faulkner's LIGHT IN AUGUST in her lap. My father was a musician who probably never read a book of fiction in his life. I put a photograph of him taken by my mother along the Alabama coastline when the two of them were snowbirding on one of the covers of my books and he looked at himself there then said to my mother, "Gee whiz, Lu, I wish I had worn another hat." But his trills on his clarinet in his den--they found their way into the way I put a sentence together in my poems, I think. My teacher in college, Dave Evans, played no small part in my development as a poet. Among many other things, Dave showed me why concision and the image are so crucial to the success of a good poem.

Are you spiritual or religious? If you are, how does that enter the poetry?

This is a question that probably should be asked of someone other than me but I will give you a hint: religions are mostly stupid because like all ideologies they think they all have it figured out. I said "mostly stupid" because the lost of the world often find refuge in religion and I would be a fool if I were to be anything but sympathetic toward a mother, say, whose daughter has been raped and murdered and who finds spiritual consolation in prayer and in the church.

Do you consider yourself a 'nature poet?'

I have always hated the phrase "nature poet." Read Theodore Roethke's short early poem "The Heron" and you will get a good idea of what it really means to be, ugh, a nature poet. That said, there has been, for me at least, a lifelong struggle going on between my fascination with and love for our world of blossoms and silkworms and morning deer in the yard and lions and tigers and bears and my often crushing disappointment with the way my brothers and sisters on planet earth behave. James Wright's poem "To A Blossoming Pear Tree" explains far better this essential quarrel with oneself. His poem concludes 'The dark blood in my body drags me down with my brother." I am not sure it could be any other way.

How important are animals in your life and poetry?

I like it when I look into an animal's eyes. I saw a snake crossing a dirt road in Tennessee years ago that turned its slender head and looked ever so briefly at me. I have looked into the eyes of turtles and had my look returned. Have you ever looked into the rolling eyes of a horse? Sometimes my last old dog and I would get lost for a good long time in one another's eyes. Jane Goodall has a chapter in her THROUGH A WINDOW where she refutes the notion that to look directly into the eyes of a chimpanzee is threatening. Looked at with love and love is returned. This is why in part I am drawn again and again in my poems to those creatures that inhabit the earth with us and, alas, depend on our understanding of them to survive. "The donkey brays like a pump gone dry." That is Elizabeth Bishop. "Humpbacked bees in pirate pants." That is John Ciardi in one of his poems. Those who do not consider themselves to be a nature poet do not know what they are missing. Even Baudelaire described a dead pig on its back alongside the road as looking "like a whore with its legs up in the air."

What is poetry's place in culture and society?

Good poems have no place to abide in America right now. Future generations will have to look for the reclusive Emily Dickenson among us who went on writing against the most compelling of odds. Who is it once said that "indifference is the one sin that most brings the angels to tears"? The poet barks in our day and age and the caravan moves on.

What are your thoughts regarding the public performance of poetry?

Poems are a performance of the written word. There is no getting around that. Marvell's first line of his famous poem "If we had but world enough and time" makes it clear that what will follow will be a performance. Same goes for Ammons' "I know if I find you I will have to leave the earth" and Donne's "Batter my heart, three-person'd god." You try to find as a poet the right ingress into the event of the poem, knowing, as Dickenson did, that "the first line is god given. You have to do the rest for yourself." Performance poetry with open mikes in bars . . . a fine time I guess for all. I have been to a couple of those performances and have left them wanting to slit my throat. I am reminded of how Auden responded after being asked when he was in America what he thought of Dylan-- that he thought the questioner had asked about Dylan Thomas and not the troubadour Bob Dylan who would get the goddamn Nobel Prize well down the line. If anything signaled the end of the world it was that. So, when the subject of poetry as a performance is brought up I don't think of young folks screaming horseshit from behind a podium in the smoky dark but of what I have tried to speak to above. The drama of poetry. Poems that in being dramatic do not forget the simple beauty of the human voice.

How does teaching co-exist with poetry?

There are two poems in my new book, WHAT MORE COULD THE UNIVERSE WANT, that address what might be a conflict between the teaching of literature and the writing of one's own poems. Those two poems are "The Russian," about a reading given by poet Joseph Brodsky to graduate students at the University of Alabama and "Those Beautiful People in The Room." I couldn't add anything to that that wouldn't sound like whining.

www.ingramcontent.com/pod-product-compliance
Lightning Source LLC
Chambersburg PA
CBHW030347100526
44592CB00010B/870